Hydrangea

R

Carnat

Mimosa

Lilies

Euphorbia

Freesias

Orchids

Tiger Lilies

Delphiniums

Viole

Ivy

Irises

Daffodils

Tu

Peonies

Anemones

THE *Flower Arranger's* HANDBOOK

THE *Flower Arranger's* HANDBOOK

CRESCENT BOOKS
NEW YORK • AVENEL, NEW JERSEY

CLB 4113
This edition published in 1994 by
Crescent Books, distributed by
Outlet Book Company, Inc., a
Random House Company
40 Engelhard Avenue, Avenel, New
Jersey 07001

Random House
New York • Toronto • London •
Sydney • Auckland

©1994 CLB Publishing Ltd,
Godalming, Surrey
Printed and bound in Singapore
All rights reserved
ISBN 0-517-120526
87654321

Managing Editor: Jo Finnis

Editors: Geraldine Christy;
Sue Wilkinson

Original Design Concept:
Nigel Duffield

Designer: Jill Coote

Photographer: Neil Sutherland

Typesetting: Julie Smith

Production: Ruth Arthur;
Sally Connolly; Neil Randles;
Karen Staff Jonathan Tickner;
Matthew Dale

Director of Production:
Gerald Hughes

Contents

Introduction

Flowers make a delightful impact on an important occasion; a wedding, christening or homecoming will become a treasured memory with a cleverly arranged display of fresh flowers. This is a good time to go to town with the arrangement using a larger vase, or a different kind of container to make an impact. Perhaps you could consider using more unusual flowers too, or use many more of your favourite flowers in a different way.

LEFT: *Golden daffodils add a bright and cheery touch to any room. Placing the flowers in a coloured vase offers additional scope especially if you choose a vase which picks out both the colours of the flowers and the colours in your room.*

Nothing seems to brighten up a room more than a dazzling display of fresh flowers. However, in reality, some of the most stunning displays are very easy to achieve and cost very little – especially during the summer months when you can pick the flowers you need for your display from your garden.

The key to a good flower display is the way the flowers are positioned and combined in an appropriate container, and once you have built up confidence handling any delicate flowers you will soon find you are happy attempting more difficult displays. Soon you will have stunning flower arrangements in the home on a regular basis.

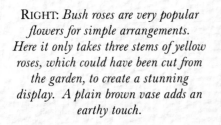

RIGHT: *Bush roses are very popular flowers for simple arrangements. Here it only takes three stems of yellow roses, which could have been cut from the garden, to create a stunning display. A plain brown vase adds an earthy touch.*

LEFT: *Here, five simple, but stunning arrangements are achieved with only a small number of flowers. In fact any one of these arrangements would look wonderful on its own, but grouped together they present a charming display. Coloured glass vases are perfect for this simple style of arrangement.*

Preparing fresh flowers

Fresh flowers will repay a little time and effort on their preparation with a long and colourful life in an arrangement. If you buy flowers from a good market stall or flower shop the chances are that they will have been conditioned. This means that stems will have been cleaned of foliage and re-cut, then stood in water for several hours to have a long drink. The stems on flowers bought in a bunch out of water will have dried and possibly sealed over and will need to be cut again and given a drink.

Flowers picked from a garden should also be given this preparatory treatment, preferably in the evening or early morning, which are the best times of the day to gather material before too much moisture has transpired from the plant. Normal soft stems should be cut at a long slant to give the largest surface area possible to absorb water. A few very large flowers, such as delphiniums and amaryllis, have hollow stems which can be packed with a small plug of damp cotton wool to help them to drink.

Some flowers and foliage have stems that need to be seared or sealed to prevent them drooping or dropping petals. Poppies are one variety that needs to have this done. Each stem should be

RIGHT: *All flowers need some preparation before they are placed in a vase. Here any foliage which will be below water should be removed. You can simply pull the foliage off, or use a sharp knife to clean the stem. Any leaves which are submerged will cloud the water and give it an unpleasant smell.*

BELOW: *Although they look lovely, tulips are supposed to be difficult flowers to display in fresh arrangements, as they quickly wilt. However, they can be quickly revived with a little boiling water. Leave them to stand in the water as long as necessary.*

12

held over a flame for a few seconds or stood in a shallow depth of boiling water for two or three minutes. Other varieties that need the heat treatment are euphorbia and some ferns.

Boiling water can also revive wilting stems of flowers such as tulips, sunflowers, gerbera and mallow. Pour a small amount of boiling water into a narrow-necked container and stand the flowers in this until they are revived.

Any foliage that is not wanted on a stem, or that will be below water, should be removed. Submerged leaves rapidly cloud the water and make it smell and look unpleasant. Some flowers, such as stocks should always have stems cleaned of foliage that might rot.

Preparing shrubby material

Many flowers and most of the foliage used in flower arranging comes from shrubby plants with strong stems which need slightly different treatment from soft-stemmed annual or herbaceous flowers. Flowers such as lilac are cut from large shrubs or small trees and their stems have bark over a solid woody stem. Preparation of this sort of material is necessary to get the best from it. The base of the stems should be cut on a slant and the bark can be scraped or peeled back a little way to expose the stem beneath. Then either split the stem by cutting a few slices upwards with sharp secateurs or a gardening knife, or hammer the bottom few centimetres with a mallet.

Once more it is important to remove unwanted leaves and small, twiggy branches that might get in the way of the arrangement or that otherwise would stand under water. Give all woody-stemmed material a good, long conditioning drink in water at room temperature and leave in a cool place until you need to use it. Some foliage can be completely submerged in water for several hours, which makes it very crisp and unlikely to wilt later.

ABOVE: *It is best to remove the thorns from roses before trying to arrange them. You can buy rose varieties which are thornless.*

RIGHT: *Woody stems need to be split to help them to take up the water. One way of splitting the stem is to hammer the bottom few centimetres with a mallet. Work on a chopping block to avoid damaging any work surfaces.*

RIGHT: *Remove any branches which might get in the way of the arrangement with secateurs. Trim any branches which overpower the arrangement at this stage too.*

BELOW: *Another method of splitting woody stems is to cut the stem using sharp secateurs or a gardening knife. This has the effect of increasing the stem's surface area.*

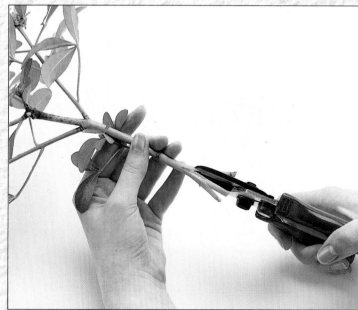

Leaves such as beech, hornbeam, and whitebeam, which you might use in a large-scale arrangement, benefit very much from this type of treatment. A large container is obviously required and a bath is usually the best place to do this conditioning.

Roses need much the same treatment, but if they have large or sharp thorns it is sensible to remove these before trying to arrange them. Roses bought from a flower shop will usually have been de-thorned and nowadays many varieties are thornless. It is a slow job cutting off each thorn, but you can try running a blade or special tool along the stem, rubbing off the thorns as you go. Roses can suddenly and dramatically wilt for no apparent reason, but can often be saved by re-cutting stems and standing in boiling water.

Simple arrangements

as teapots, cake moulds and boxes can easily take on a new lease of life. Collect small bottles, glasses of different shapes and types, interesting jars, bowls and jugs ranging from the functional to the highly decorative. Bunches of blooms used generously will provide stunning results every time.

If you intend to use a basket for fresh flowers then you will have to use an inner container, or line it with plastic to take advantage of the easy-to-use floral foams which are ideal for this method of display.

LEFT: *A coffee pot makes a wonderful container for this bunch of pretty pink scabious. Leaving the lid next to the pot adds to the informal effect.*

RIGHT: *Wicker baskets make great containers for flower arrangements. Remember to line the basket with a waterproof layer – a plastic bag will do the trick – then add florist's foam and your flowers.*

A simple arrangement or two makes a big difference to how a house looks and feels. Try to find time to put together a quick bunch of cheerful flowers for a kitchen table and something welcoming in the hall or living room. These arrangements do not need to be elaborate, but should provide a splash of colour – something fresh and alive– and if possible add the bonus of a delicious scent.

Many people are nervous about flower arranging, imagining that there are rules to keep and styles to follow. Forget all this and go for something as simple as possible. Search around for all kinds of different containers to inspire your flower arranging. Ordinary household objects such

LEFT: *Anemones are so vivid they really need no further adornment. Here, they are cleverly grouped in a clear glass vase, providing a perfect table-top display.*

Special occasions

one time circlets of evergreens were commonly used to decorate houses at Christmas, but now there are few occasions when garlands and wreaths would not fit in. A flower wreath can be made on a damp foam or moss base and easy garlands can be put together using wire alone.

LEFT: *A small arrangement of dahlias and chrysanthemums make a lovely dinner table centrepiece. Set in a small bowl this display will provide a good talking point without hiding the guests.*

Good food deserves beautiful flowers to set the scene. A dining table looks finished and inviting with some kind of flower centrepiece. Flowers can be chosen to complement or contrast with the food, to echo a colour in plates or table linen, or simply to work within the whole room. Bear in mind that people need room to eat and to see and talk easily to other guests. Keep centrepieces fairly low and though fragrant flowers are pleasing, choose nothing too scented which might clash with the food.

Posies are one of the simplest ways to arrange flowers and they make an ideal gift for all kinds of occasions. Traditionally, posies are carried by a bride and her attendants and in Victorian times were given as love tokens and taken to grand balls and parties as decoration for beautiful gowns. A well-made posy can be stood in water as a ready-made flower arrangement.

In recent years we have become used to seeing garlands and wreaths at all times of the year. At

RIGHT: *One of the best tricks for displaying fresh flowers in a clear glass vase is to use glass beads. These allow the flower arranger to position each stem accurately, like florist's foam, with the added advantage of being colourless.*

18

RIGHT: *Three stems of amaryllis and some small flowered orchids provide a superb arrangement for a special occasion. The background height has been set with a few stems of twiggy foliage.*

Roses

*T*he rose is one of the most useful and outstanding of cut flowers. Everyone's favourite, it can be used for many types of arrangement, from the formal and sophisticated to a simple jug or basket. The colour range is vast and there is a wide variety of flower shapes and textures, with the bonus that many roses have beautiful almost heavenly fragrances.

Choose from garden-grown roses and cultivated ones both have their strong points. Roses from the flower shop come in a slightly limited colour range, often with long straight stems which are useful for large-scale arrangements. Garden roses are fuller petalled but short stemmed and usually have scent as well as coming in a wide choice of colours.

Roses repay careful initial preparation so always re-cut their woody stems and split the base a little way up to help them drink water. Strip thorns if they will be a nuisance when arranging the blooms and take off foliage unless it is specifically part of the overall design. Roses are happy arranged in water or floral foam and last up to 10 days.

RIGHT: **1** *Make a small bundle of damp moss in your hand and bind it together with mossing wire, criss-crossing to secure.*

FAR RIGHT: **2** *Lay the moss bundle on a quarter of the twigs, then add more twigs to completely enclose the moss. The twigs should be roughly the same length.*

ABOVE: **3** *Tie round the centre of the twig bundle with strong wire to hold everything in place. You may need help to hold the twigs while you do this.*

ABOVE: **4** *Begin to push stems of roses into the ends of the twig bundle, making sure that all of the cut stems are in contact with the damp moss.*

ABOVE: **5** *Continue adding roses of varying stem length to complete the bundle. Finish off with a wide gauzy bow round the middle of the bundle to hide the wire.*

BELOW: *The finished twig and rose bundle looks lovely hanging from a long ribbon against a door or wall.*

Roses

ABOVE: **1** *Cut off most of the lower leaves along six stems of tall yellow roses. Do the same with three dahlia stems.*

ABOVE: **2** *Carefully spread out a bunch of long narrow leaves. These are from an iris variety. Fan them out slightly on the surface.*

ABOVE: **3** *Start to lay the longest rose stems on top of the leaves, placing the flower heads where the leaves start to fan out.*

RIGHT: **4** *Add the rest of the roses, then the three dahlias, making an even and well-spaced effect. Trim off stems at base if necessary.*

LEFT: *This elegant bunch would make a stunning decoration or gift to stand in a plain glass vase.*

ABOVE: **5** *Tie the bunch loosely with string or wire, then wrap a wide gauze ribbon over the wire and finish with a large bow.*

RIGHT: *This arrangement would look equally good made with any colour rose, but long-stemmed varieties give the best effect.*

ABOVE: **4** *Trim the lower leaves of eight stems of roses leaving a few leaves above the level of the vase. Put all the roses in amongst the twigs.*

ABOVE: **3** *Put a small amount of water in a plain glass container. Place groups of twigs inside container leaning them at different angles against the sides.*

ABOVE: **1** *Trim away all leaves from some straight twigs. These twigs are from a dogwood shrub and have attractive red bark.*

LEFT: **2** *Cut the clean twigs to a reasonable length for your container. They need not all be exactly the same length.*

ABOVE: **1** *Soak a piece of floral foam which has been used to fill a shallow oblong container. Cut extra pieces to fit if needed.*

ABOVE: **2** *Prepare rose hips by snipping short stems off a large branch. Then push a stiff stub wire up into each stem to lengthen it.*

ABOVE: **3** *Trim off the lower stems and leaves from a bunch of yellow solidago or a similar flower to use as a filler.*

ABOVE: *A wonderful autumn mixture made using unexpected combinations of fruit and flowers.*

RIGHT: **6** *Now put the orchids, rose hips and a few other pieces such as crab apples and chrysanthemums throughout the filler.*

ABOVE: **4** *Now snip small pieces of orange orchid from a large spray, each with about two to three blooms along its length.*

ABOVE: **5** *Start to push the small pieces of solidago into the damp foam aiming to fill the whole container with one layer.*

LEFT: **1** *With a sharp knife cut damp floral foam into wedge shapes which can be packed into a plastic-lined heart-shaped basket.*

RIGHT: **2** *Cut small sprigs of borage with flowers and just a few small leaves left at the base. Push them into the foam to completely cover it.*

ABOVE: *A basket like this one looks pretty seen from above, so it is best displayed on a low surface or propped up slightly to show off the shape.*

BELOW: **3** *Now begin to add yellow rose heads cut quite short from their stems. Space the flowers out evenly across the heart basket.*

25

Gerbera

Gerbera are bright colourful flowers which come originally from South Africa. They are sometimes called Transvaal Daisy and are very useful for flower arrangements where bold simple shapes and strong colours are required. The colours range from cream, peach, pale pink and yellow to deep scarlet, orange and crimson.

Gerbera stems are very long and should stay stiff without the flower heads bending too much. Sometimes there are problems with the blooms as they exude a bacteria from the stems which pollutes the water. Always use a cut flower food and conditioner in the vase which has first been cleaned with a mild bleach.

Gerbera look very good used alone in a single colour for bold, fresh-looking arrangements or used as important flowers in mixed and more classical designs. The strong colours are particularly useful as there are few other cut flowers with such dramatic presence. There are single varieties and some doubles which have an extra ring of smaller petals around the central eye.

ABOVE: **1** *Find a small ready-made gift carrier bag as here and stand a container of some kind inside which will hold water or damp foam.*

RIGHT: **2** *You will need eight cerise pink gerbera and a collection of other flowers such as cornflower, daisies and dill. Trim their stalks.*

FAR RIGHT: **3** *Begin to loosely fill the container with the secondary flowers, spreading them equally and facing the daisies towards the front of the bag.*

ABOVE: **4** *Check you are happy with the effect of the secondary flowers by turning the gift bag around so you can see the effect from all angles.*

LEFT: **5** *Trim the gerbera stems to the right length and start to put them in amongst the other flowers, spacing them equally working from side to side.*

ABOVE: *This makes a pretty arrangement for any situation or give it as a ready-made floral present using foam instead of water.*

Gerbera

ABOVE: **1** *Cut one block of soaked floral foam horizontally into two pieces and stand them one in front of the other.*

ABOVE: **2** *Make small bent pins from a reel of wire. Collect laurel leaves of the same size and attach them to edge of foam with pins, overlapping each one.*

ABOVE: **3** *Now tie a length of green string or garden twine around the centre of the leaves and take at least three turns. Tie it securely at the back.*

ABOVE: *The finished arrangement looks wonderful as a table centrepiece and you could of course adapt this design to different dimensions to suit you.*

BELOW: **4** *You will need nine large-flowered gerbera. Cut off their stems very short as the heads will sit right against the foam.*

BELOW: **5** *Space them absolutely equally in three rows, starting with a centre flower. As long as the flowers are all the same size this will work.*

ABOVE: **1** *For this idea you will need a glass cylinder and a piece of bamboo on a roll. Cut the bamboo to fit and wrap around the vase.*

ABOVE: **2** *To fix the bamboo in place use two small pieces of strong wire and twist the bamboo together at top and bottom.*

ABOVE: *This colour scheme is effective but you could also use contrasting ribbon colours or different colours of flower and ribbon mixed together.*

ABOVE: **3** *Now cut enough pieces of ribbon for a bow for each gerbera. You will need from six to a dozen flowers according to budget.*

RIGHT: **4** *Stand each flower into place in the vase and tie a small bow around the very top of the stem under the flower head.*

29

Lilac

*L*ilac is a shrub with woody stems and sprays of beautiful flowers made up of hundreds of small trumpet-shaped blooms. It comes in shades of purple, mauve and white in single and double varieties. When grown commercially it is forced to flower earlier than it would do outdoors. This process sadly rids the forced kinds of their magnificent scent.

Long-stemmed flowers like lilac are very useful for large-scale and spectacular arrangements and, if the stems are carefully treated, blooms should last for up to a fortnight. Most of the forced crop is white early in the season. Later, more mauve lilac appears and then the outdoor grown supplies come in. Always split the woody stems a little to help them take up water. Use a cut flower food and change water frequently to help the blooms last.

Lilac is always sold with the leaves removed from the stems. If you pick your own strip off the foliage which otherwise might droop and take precious moisture from the flowers. Mauve and purple varieties of lilac look lovely mixed with green, apricot, pink and even deep red.

ABOVE: **1** *Make a sausage shape from some damp moss and bind it round with mossing wire to make a firm basis for the twigs.*

RIGHT: **2** *Begin to put the twigs around the moss shape, which should be at one end of the bundle. You may need to tie the twigs before finishing.*

FAR RIGHT: **3** *Cut each stem of lilac a little way up from the base with sharp secateurs to help it take up moisture.*

RIGHT: **4** *Make sure bundle is tied firmly at lower end with wire, then start to push the lilac stems down into moss at base of bundle.*

ABOVE: **5** *When all the twigs are in place tie thin ribbon to cover wire at base of bundle, then add a decorative rosette or bow to ribbon.*

LEFT: *This twig bundle can stay as it is lying on a flat surface or it can stand upright, balanced if necessary, or in a basket or other container.*

LEFT: *This little flower-edged basket would make a lovely get-well present or a thank you to someone special. Vary the contents to suit the recipient.*

BELOW: **4** *Now fill the basket with multi-coloured sugared almonds, piling them up so that they show above the flowers around the edge.*

ABOVE: **2** *Work round the top of the basket tying in alternate lilac and ranunculus using the wire attached to each bloom.*

RIGHT: **3** *Continue working round in one direction until the top edge is completely surrounded and you have a thick collar of flowers.*

ABOVE: **1** *You first need to wire all the ranunculus flowers and sprigs of lilac in order to be able to attach them to the basket.*

LEFT: **2** *When the basic lilac bunch is finished start to add some dark purple anemones and pink roses carefully around the central bunch.*

RIGHT: **3** *Now bind the stems of the complete bunch tightly together. It is important to make a strong well-wired handle to the posy as a base for the ribbon.*

ABOVE: **1** *Begin to make a posy in the hand with a combination of lilac sprays and Michaelmas daisies. Leave the stalks at a medium length.*

BELOW: **4** *Now make a gold ribbon rosette and attach it to a length of stub wire. Push the wire up into the posy stems.*

BELOW: **5** *Take a length of silver ribbon and wrap this down the stems working in a spiral. Tuck the end under the spiral.*

ABOVE: *The finished posy has an old-fashioned, almost Elizabethan, feel to it and would make a beautiful bouquet for a bridesmaid to carry.*

LEFT: **6** *Starting at the bottom, above the rosette, wind gold cord up the handle criss-crossing it, then knot the end.*

Delphiniums

*A*s true blue flowers are quite scarce the delphinium in all its forms is one of the most popular cut flowers. Some of the tallest varieties are almost too large for most flower arrangements, but provide height and sense of occasion where there is room. Annual varieties, usually known as larkspur, make wonderful summer bouquets and dry well too.

Delphiniums are flowers of summer gardens but these days they are grown commercially and available for most months of the year. They can last from eight to twelve days as cut flowers and are generally used with a mixture of other flowers rather than on their own. They come in a wonderful range of blues from palest silvery mauve and light turquoise to deep sky blue and velvety Prussian blue, some with a pale and others a dark central eye. Annual larkspur also comes in pink and peach shades and there is a white variety of both perennial and annual types too.

Always remove the small leaves which grow along the lower stems to avoid polluting the water they are in and use a cut flower food to prolong their life.

ABOVE: **1** *Put a small amount of water in the jug. It does not have to be very deep but always keep it topped up. Add first stems of delphiniums.*

BELOW: **4** *Fill any gaps with more roses, dill and larkspur until the jug looks filled and balanced. Finish off with a light spray of water to freshen the arrangement.*

BELOW: **2** *Now add some aquilegia or similar flowers of the same height beside them and at the back of the jug, then add a bunch of spray roses.*

ABOVE: *This would look good with some light shining through the deep blue jug, so stand the finished arrangement with a light source behind it.*

RIGHT: **3** *Add a few more soft bushy flowers such as dill or cow parsley and prepare three red peonies, stripping off their lower leaves.*

Delphiniums

RIGHT: **1** *Cut out a centre core of apple to leave a small space to fill with flowers. Take a small slice from base too if needed for apple to stand upright.*

FAR RIGHT: **2** *Fill each apple with a little water. You may need to top this up regularly to keep flowers fresh.*

RIGHT: **3** *Cut stems of flowers such as delphiniums into very small pieces or single flowers. Rose stems should just be cut short. Put them into apple vases.*

BELOW: *Group a few apples together – three or more for the best effect – and fill them with a mixture of flowers or flowers of one type.*

ABOVE: **1** *Cut floral foam to closely fit a narrow basket or other container. You will probably need to line a basket first with thin plastic or foil.*

ABOVE: **2** *Prepare the flowers so that each type is of exactly the same length. The delphiniums should be the tallest.*

LEFT: **3** *Make a first back row of delphiniums, then make a row of white antirrhinums in front of these. Next add red roses in a third row.*

ABOVE: *Finish off with a neat row of laurel leaves at the front of the basket and trim away any small flowers on the lower stems.*

Peonies

Peonies are one of the most glamorous of summer flowers. Their enormous many-petalled heads add substance and rich colours to any flower arrangement. Their season is very brief and falls in early summer alongside many other beautiful garden flowers which combine so well with them.
Pink and red varieties are most commonly seen but there are white ones too. Cut blooms as they begin to open and lay flat in a dry, cool place for 24 hours to prevent petal drop.

Luckily, peonies have good strong stems to support their heavy heads but tend to need floral foam or wire in containers to help keep them in place. They are usually picked in bud and when bought should show some colour but be tightly closed. They open slowly and then last for up to two weeks. There are single varieties, some with attractive golden stamens in the centre of the bloom, but most commercial types are fully double with wonderful wavy-edged petals.

Surprisingly, peonies dry very well if hung in a warm airy place and can then be used in winter arrangements. Some varieties have a sweet fragrance but it is for their texture, colour and shape that peonies are mostly used.

BELOW: **1** *A rustic basket suits this garden-inspired summer mixture. Tape damp floral foam level to top of basket.*

LEFT: **2** *Begin to make an outline fan shape at back and sides of basket with the tallest material such as larkspur, delphiniums and catmint.*

BELOW: **3** *Next, working in front of the first layer, add some solid flowers such as spikes of stock, phlox and sweet williams.*

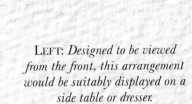

LEFT: *Designed to be viewed from the front, this arrangement would be suitably displayed on a side table or dresser.*

RIGHT: **4** *Finally, add the peony blooms, facing them forwards and well spaced out. Fill in any gaps with lighter blooms such as sweet peas.*

Peonies

RIGHT: **2** *Snip the heads of two peonies and one rose from their stems, leaving a centimetre of stalk. Choose flowers in shades of one colour.*

BELOW: **3** *Gently place the large flower heads into the bowl, being careful not to soak the lower petals too much. The heads will float and stay fresh.*

ABOVE: **1** *This is a very quick and easy idea. Fill a round straight-sided bowl with water. Float some rose petals on the surface.*

RIGHT: *This idea is excellent for a party or dinner table. It looks pretty from above and through the sides of the glass bowl.*

LEFT: **1** *This ideas relies on carefully chosen components. Fill a sparkling clean fish bowl with water and add clear glass marbles.*

RIGHT: *This is a strong and stylish arrangement and it needs careful positioning in a light place with simple, uncluttered surroundings.*

ABOVE: **2** *Trim off the white and muddy lower stems from a bunch of bear grass. Keep the rubber band in place which holds the grass together.*

ABOVE: **3** *Put the grass still in its band to one side of vase. Next add an artichoke leaf and hellebore leaf or similar, then an allium flower head.*

ABOVE: **4** *Finally position a single deep red peony head at the front and to the right of the vase. Reposition any of the other pieces, if necessary.*

Freesias

Freesias are justifiably popular for their range of colours, their good keeping properties once cut, and not least their wonderful scent. They are often bought as a gift for they are always a delight to receive and are usefully available all the year round. Bunches are often sold made from a mixture of colours but it is possible to buy them in single colours too.

The first flower on the stem should be open when bought and then the other flower buds along the stem will open in sequence. Pick off dead flowers as they finish. Freesias have stiff stems which make them easy to arrange in water or foam. Add a little sugar to the water to improve the length of time that they are in bloom.

Freesias are available in white, cream, yellow, mauve, orangey reds and crimson. Grown from a bulb, there are outdoor types but commercially most crops are grown under glass. Freesias can be mixed with other flowers but also look lovely displayed alone. The highly scented white and cream varieties are often used in bridal bouquets and wedding flowers.

ABOVE: **1** *Choose a round and fairly upright basket or bowl for this design. If you use a basket it will need to be lined with a sheet of plastic.*

ABOVE: **2** *Now soak a block of floral foam and push this into place inside the basket. Start to add stems of variegated foliage such as euphorbia cut to length.*

ABOVE: **3** *Continue adding more foliage such as euonymus across the whole basket so that the foam is completely covered. Check you are happy with the effect at this stage.*

ABOVE: **4** *Next put some stems of a scented white narcissi such as 'Paperwhite' in amongst the foliage to add contrast and fragrance.*

ABOVE: **5** *Stems of deep pink roses are used next. Spread these throughout the arrangement to give a balanced effect.*

ABOVE: *The freesias give a wonderful scent and provide an unusual colour combination with the deep pink roses. Try yellow freesias with peach or orange roses.*

ABOVE: **6** *Finally put stems of deep mauve freesias in. Balance the spaces between the blooms and make sure to put some stems near the edge of the basket.*

Freesias

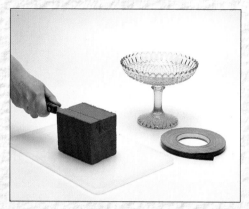

ABOVE: **1** *Cut a block of floral foam into a piece which will fit the glass dish. It should not be too high. Soak the foam.*

ABOVE: **2** *Put the foam into place and then tape it firmly to the dish with two strips of florists' tape crossing in the middle.*

ABOVE: **3** *Cover the foam with stems of foliage. Here variegated periwinkle has been used and allowed to bend gracefully.*

ABOVE: **4** *Cut small sprigs of Michaelmas daisy and put these throughout the foam, making a rounded shape to the outline. Add a few Ornithogolum arabicum.*

RIGHT: *This is a fairly formal arrangement which would look good on a tallish piece of furniture or perhaps used as a table centrepiece.*

RIGHT: **5** *Now put mauve freesias throughout the arrangement, spacing them evenly to make a balanced and symmetrical shape and keeping the outline smooth.*

ABOVE: *This idea works best as a group of three or more bags together. Angle them however you like, but keep them quite close to each other for the best effect.*

ABOVE: **1** *You will need some small paper bags designed for wrapping gifts. These are gold foil. They must be big enough to hold tumblers inside.*

ABOVE: **2** *Pour a little water into each tumbler in the bags, then begin by putting some white narcissi into the bags. These add bulk and more fragrance.*

ABOVE: **3** *Add stems of freesias to the narcissi. Here mauve, yellow and white varieties were used. The flowers should be just above top edge of bags.*

Tulips

*G*arden tulips are very seasonal flowers appearing through spring, but these days early blooms are available through the winter too. The choice of colours is very wide and there are different types such as multi-flowered, fringed parrot tulips and double varieties as well as the tall-stemmed simple types most people know. Tulips are wonderful for informal arrangements, but can be used in planned displays too.

Tulips have a reputation for being slightly difficult to handle. The main point to remember is that even once cut, they twist and turn towards the light and even appear to go on growing. Any arrangement must therefore accommodate this.

Occasionally tulips droop dramatically before they have even been used. You can often rescue them by re-cutting their stems, wrapping them tightly in paper and standing them in hot water for a while. They can be exceptionally long lived as cut flowers and add colour and shape like no other flower to an arrangement. Bunch them simply into a glass jug or tank or add fewer blooms to a mixed arrangement for a Dutch Old Master effect.

RIGHT: *Stand the finished display on a gold paper doily and scatter a few extra fruits at the base of the arrangement. This would look beautiful on a hall table or sideboard.*

LEFT: **1** *Soak a block of floral foam and attach it to a stemmed plate with florists' adhesive tape. Use as little as possible to leave room for stems.*

RIGHT: **2** *Begin to make a layer of fruits around the base of the foam right round the dish. Here apricots and golden plums were used.*

ABOVE: **3** *Pile a few more fruits on top of the foam, then add some longish stems of orange orchid and three stems of Leucospermum.*

ABOVE: **4** *Open out the seed pods of some Cape gooseberries (Physalis) to expose the pretty orange fruits inside them. Leave a few just slightly opened.*

ABOVE: **5** *Add the fruits to the arrangement and finally several tulips in shades of orange and apricot, filling in any spaces between the fruits and other flowers.*

Tulips

RIGHT: **1** *You will need two glass containers, one large and one small, to stand beside each other. Trim flower stems to fit and remove lower part of hyacinth stems.*

BELOW: *Two vases together create greater impact than one alone. Here the scale is quite different in flowers and containers.*

ABOVE: **2** *Put water into both vases. Arrange the tulips and hyacinths quite loosely and casually into the larger container. Leave a few green leaves on the tulips.*

ABOVE: **3** *Now concentrate on the smaller container. Cut a bunch of grape hyacinth and yellow narcissi to the right length. Arrange each type of flower in little groups.*

RIGHT: *These strong colours are unusual for a spring arrangement but would look particularly good against a dark polished wood or rich fabric background.*

ABOVE: **1** *Fit a piece of damp floral foam into a lined round basket. Cut the stems of striped red and cream tulips and red ranunculus to remove lower leaves.*

ABOVE: **2** *Push the stems of tulips and ranunculus gently into the foam. Make a start to the hole in the foam with a stick if necessary.*

ABOVE: **3** *Once you have filled the basket all over with flowers so that it looks good from all round, cover the foam which shows with small pieces of fresh moss.*

Ranunculus

Ranunculus have deservedly grown in popularity over the last few years as a colourful and long-lasting cut flower. They manage to be both unsophisticated and yet classy with their round flower heads packed with layer upon layer of papery petals. They are available nearly all the year round these days with peaks in December, March and April.

Ranunculus are very pretty at the bud stage before the flower opens out completely and also once their petals are totally open, when they look like small peonies. Some types are more simple than others with the central eye and stamens showing well, but what is pleasing about them all is the variation between flowers in a single bunch. The colour range is tremendous, from white to brilliant buttercup yellow and glossy orange through all the reds and pinks. There are some versions with pretty feathery lines in darker colours traced over the petals.

The stems can be a little weak or bent, but treated carefully the blooms can last up to two weeks. Surprisingly, they also dry well, but the stems need to be wired.

RIGHT: *The finished wreath can be hung on a door or wall, or laid horizontally on a flat surface to make a table centrepiece.*

LEFT: **1** *Use a ready-made foam wreath ring for this idea and soak it thoroughly. Cut the stems of foliage and flowers very short.*

ABOVE: **2** *Start to put the small pieces of euphorbia marginata into the wreath, working round systematically until it is evenly covered.*

ABOVE: **3** *Next put the little sprigs of pink genista in amongst the foliage, working round the wreath and placing them evenly but leaving them a little taller than the foliage.*

LEFT: **4** *Add stems of deep pink ranunculus at intervals around the ring. Finish off with a small cluster of well-opened cream roses at the bottom left of wreath.*

ABOVE: **1** *These ranunculus were brought like this as a mixed bunch in beautiful shades of pink, peach and apricot. Make a posy with them.*

ABOVE: **2** *Tie the stems together in two places with thin wire, first at the top high up under the flowers and second near the base of the stems.*

LEFT: **3** *Wind thin gold cord or string around the stems, tying it to itself at top and bottom. Trim off the stems neatly.*

ABOVE: *The bow is attached to the stems with wire just under the flower heads to add a glamorous finishing touch.*

BELOW: **4** *Get a piece of wire-edged ribbon to make a bow. Twist fine wire at the centre.*

RIGHT: **5** *While leaving the end of the wire long, loop the ribbon to give the effect of a bow and hold the loops at their base.*

FAR RIGHT: **6** *Make several more loops until ribbon is used up. With the end of wire secure the loops to each other at their bases.*

LEFT: **1** *Take a little time to gather the pieces and prepare them properly. Fill a small round bowl with damp floral foam.*

LEFT: **2** *Put the first of the cleaned stemmed ranunculus into the foam, working all round the bowl so that it looks good from every direction.*

ABOVE: **3** *Now add a few clusters of bright yellow alstromeria to add a different flower shape to the bowl.*

ABOVE: **4** *Finally small spikes of blue grape hyacinth are pushed into the arrangement, projecting a little above the other flowers.*

RIGHT: **5** *Put a blue plate behind the arrangement a little off centre. This throws the yellow flowers into relief.*

ABOVE: *An arrangement to celebrate the colours and flowers of spring. Yellow and blue always look fresh and attractive together.*

Ranunculus

ABOVE: **1** *To make this scented basket arrangement line a handled basket with plastic.*

LEFT: **2** *Cut a piece of damp floral foam to roughly fit inside the basket to come just under the basket's edge.*

RIGHT: **3** *Put several spear-shaped leaves in the foam. These are a variegated arum leaf but you could use ferns. Add some hyacinth flowers.*

ABOVE: **4** *Continue to fill the basket with a mixture of ranunculus, pale anemones and bright spray carnations.*

BELOW: **5** *Finish off the whole thing with a bright pink little bow made from wire-edged ribbon attached with wire to the handle.*

RIGHT: *This glowing ranunculus basket arrangement would make a perfect Mother's Day gift, and would also look attractive in pastel and creamy tones.*

BELOW: **1** *A terracotta pot makes an unusual container for an arrangement of eucalyptus and ranunculus. Fill with damp foam.*

BELOW: **2** *Strip the lower leaves from several stems of eucalyptus which have been cut from a larger bunch.*

ABOVE: *The blue green of the eucalyptus works as a good foil against the peach and pink shapes of the mixed ranunculus.*

RIGHT: **3** *Begin to put the eucalyptus stems into the pot, working all round it and spacing them apart equally.*

BELOW: **5** *Add the ranunculus at even spaces to make an overall balanced shape to the pot, the tallest in the centre.*

BELOW: **4** *Trim some stems of ranunculus clean of lower leaves and buds and start to put them in amongst the leaves.*

Anemones

*A*nemones are bright cheerful flowers for the darkest winter months. Usually quite inexpensive to buy and considered unsophisticated, they are nevertheless beautiful with their deep rich colours, inky black centres and velvet-textured petals. They look stunning against a simple foliage background that will project their strong colours. Often sold in bud, they quickly open in a warm and light room and last for up to twelve days.

Anemones come in white, red, pink, deep blue and purple. New larger-flowered varieties have been bred to supersede the original 'De Caen' types. Their stems are stiff and straight, making them ideal cut flowers though they are rarely tall enough for large-scale arrangements. They are normally used in posies, bouquets and medium to small-scale arrangements, where their strong colours add contrast and texture.

When they are used as a cut flower in water it pays to use flower food to prolong their flowering life. Short-stemmed anemones are normally sold in mixed-colour bunches, while the longer stemmed types are more often available as single-colour bunches. Though they feature as a winter flower they are usually available through to the summer too.

ABOVE: **1** *A ring dish is ideal for this arrangement or a metal ring mould from the kitchen. Failing that, a plate without a hole is fine. Fill with damp moss.*

ABOVE: **2** *Snip pieces of foliage from larger branches into small manageable pieces. Any fairly small-leaved garden evergreens will be suitable.*

ABOVE: **3** *The pieces of variegated euonymus and garrya elliptica should be put alternately around the dish, pushing their stems into the moss.*

ABOVE: **4** *Now put about eight to ten red anemones in amongst the foliage, spacing them out equally all around the ring.*

LEFT: *This would make a perfect Christmas table centrepiece or decoration for anywhere in the house. Of course you could vary the colour scheme if you wished.*

ABOVE: **5** *Make a ribbon rosette by looping a length of ribbon several times and then securing it with stub wire. Push this down into the centre of the ring.*

Anemones

LEFT: **1** Cut three strips of tissue paper and lay them together. Cut along one long edge to form a series of points. They do not have to be totally accurate.

RIGHT: **2** Spread out the three layers of tissue paper so that they are separated from each other and one above another but the sides should roughly match.

ABOVE: **3** Now make a bunch of mixed-colour anemones loosely in your hand or on the table. Tie the stems together about halfway along the stems.

RIGHT: This idea takes a very simple bunch of flowers and transforms it with bright tissue paper. It would make a lovely gift too, with some ribbon and a bow.

RIGHT: **4** Now start to wrap the paper around the flowers, with the points just below the flowers. Grip the paper tightly around the stems.

ABOVE: **5** *Pick up the bunch and continue wrapping the paper so that it overlaps itself. Secure the paper with another piece of string or a rubber band.*

ABOVE: **1** *Assemble a collection of paper cups and plates in a floral design, which can be the starting point for the flowers you choose to fill them.*

ABOVE: **2** *Don't put water in yet, but put small bunches of anemones and other flowers into the cups. Aim to use lots of different colours together.*

ABOVE: **6** *Stand the bunch in a small glass jar with water in it. Pull the paper points into shape so that they prettily frame the flowers.*

LEFT: **3** *Once all the flowers are in the cups and they are positioned in a group as you want them, gently pour a little water into each container.*

BELOW: *This is a bright and cheerful light-hearted arrangement suitable for a party or buffet table or even for an outdoor meal.*

Anemones

LEFT: *Stand the finished arrangement against a light background or in a window to emphasize the ribbon effect around the glass vase.*

BELOW: **4** *Now take single blooms from a bunch of purple anemones and put these in amongst the foliage and flowers in the vase. You will need eight to ten blooms.*

ABOVE: **1** *You will need a wide open-weave ribbon for this idea. It is important that the bow is semi-transparent to see the vase behind. Knot it once.*

ABOVE: **2** *Put water in the vase and start to add sprays of narrow-leaved eucalyptus. Turn the vase around to check the arrangement looks good from all angles.*

ABOVE: **3** *Once all the foliage is in place start to add a few sprays of mauve statice and Michaelmas daisy, both roughly the same height.*

BELOW: **1** *As the box is made from card you will need to put a watertight container inside it. Into this put a block of damp foam to support the flowers.*

LEFT: **2** *Start to put some tall branches of foliage into the foam. This is all from winter evergreen shrubs including some flowering viburnum tinus.*

BELOW: **3** *Once you have put all the foliage in place then stand the bowl inside the box and continue working on it while it is in situ.*

ABOVE: **4** *Now add a generous amount of long stemmed white and bi-coloured red and white anemones, spreading them equally throughout the foliage and aiming for a full effect.*

ABOVE: *If you wish you can lean the hat box lid against the side of the arrangement once it is in its final position. The hat box is large and will need a big table or piece of furniture to accommodate it.*

Sweet Peas

Sweet peas are quite short lived as a cut flower but they are still one of the most popular summer flowers to grow and buy for arrangements. Their wonderful mix of bright and pastel colours, combined with a sensational fragrance, has put them at the top of many people's favourite flower list. Sweet peas are easily grown from seed and produce masses of flowers continuously throughout the summer months.

Early forced blooms grown under glass are available from late spring and then from early summer onwards outdoor crops come on tap right through to the early autumn. Sweet peas are a tall annual plant which have to grow up supports. They produce dozens of blooms. Each long stiff flower stem carries up to six flowers, sometimes with frilled edges, sometimes with plain. The colour range is vast with every colour except yellow, orange and green. There are deepest burgundies, vivid scarlets, pale pinks, bright salmons and cool blues and mauves.

Some varieties are much more scented than others, but all are decorative either used alone or with other flowers. Condition blooms well before arranging them, then they should last up to a week.

RIGHT: *Finish off by tying a soft bow and ribbon around the stem of the posy, especially if the flowers are to be carried as wedding flowers.*

ABOVE: **1** *Make a posy up in the hand from a mixture of sweet peas, fresh lavender and Michaelmas daisies. Tie the stems with wire and trim the ends.*

ABOVE: **2** *Take a coloured doily to make a collar for the posy. Fold it in half across the middle and then in half across the radius. Cut out a central hole.*

ABOVE: **3** *Now cut the doily from the edge right into the centre. This will make it possible to overlap the edges and make a slight cone shape.*

ABOVE: **4** *Take the two cut edges and pull them towards each other, overlapping one over the other. Fix them with double-sided tape.*

ABOVE: **5** *Now put the posy through the hole in the doily and pull the collar up around the flowers. Use tape if needed to fix the doily in place.*

BELOW: 1 *This arrangement uses a very pretty miniature Victorian basket. Line the basket with moss all round the sides.*

LEFT: *This little basket would look pretty on a bedside table in a guest room or on a small round table in a living room.*

RIGHT: 2 *Put a small piece of damp floral foam in the middle of the basket. Start to put some short-stemmed roses throughout the foam.*

ABOVE: 3 *After putting about six roses in the basket fill the rest of the spaces with short cut stems of pale cream and pink sweet peas.*

LEFT: *This is a classic way of displaying sweet peas and it is still one of the best ways to appreciate blooms as each is kept separate from the next.*

ABOVE: **1** *For this classic arrangement of sweet peas you will need an old-fashioned heavy pin holder. Put this in the centre of a stemmed dish and add water.*

LEFT: **2** *Trim and prepare all the bunches of sweet peas, cutting them to roughly the same length. Mix the separate colours.*

ABOVE: **3** *Start to put sweet peas into place singly, pushing the stems between the pins in the holder. This holds them tightly at the angle you put them in.*

Cornflowers

Cornflowers are sweet and simple summer flowers. One of the few really true blue flowers, they are an annual plant and easy to grow in gardens and are commercially grown to be sold as cut flowers. Some varieties come in other colours or a mixture of different colours including pink, red, purple and white. If you grow them, pick them regularly and then more flowers will open throughout the summer.

Cornflowers have soft and rather weak stems which can make them difficult to use in foam unless cut very short. They are marvellous, though, for relaxed and informal bunches and arranged into jugs of mixed garden flowers. The deep blue colour blends well with reds, pinks, mauves and whites as well as contrasting with bright yellows and oranges. Blue is the commonest cornflower colour seen but they also come in mixed bunches with mauve, pink, burgundy and white versions.

Before arranging cornflowers clean off any small leaves, branches and unopened buds on stems which might be below water level. Use a cut flower food and change water frequently. They should last for up to a week and also dry well for winter arrangements.

LEFT: **1** *You will need a medium size ready-made twig wreath to use as a base for this garland. Snip some spikes of pink stock into small pieces.*

RIGHT: **2** *You will probably be able to simply push the sprigs of stock into the twigs and they will stay put. If not, attach them with wire.*

RIGHT: **3** *Now add scabious flower heads and put them in between the stocks, pushing the stems in amongst the twigs as before.*

The wreath will not last very long as there is no moisture for the flower stems. Keep it sprayed with water and it will last for a wedding or party.

ABOVE: **4** *Next put some small spray carnations in bright pink in amongst the other flowers, spreading them out equally round the wreath.*

RIGHT: **5** *To make the cornflowers more showy make small bunches of two or three flowers together and bind with wire. Add to the wreath.*

Cornflowers

LEFT: **2** *Cut long stems of a small-leaved variegated ivy. Push their cut stems into the foam and twine the stems round the handle.*

RIGHT: **3** *The stems will stay twined naturally if they are tied to the handle at their tips with a small piece of wire.*

ABOVE: **1** *Put a block of damp foam in a plastic-lined basket. The basket must have a tall handle.*

BELOW: *Using the ivy to decorate the basket handle makes a very simple arrangement into something quite special.*

ABOVE: **4** *Now fill the basket with something such as this unusual love-in-a-mist to cover the foam and make a filler.*

BELOW: **5** *Cut stems of cornflower to the right length and push them gently into the foam using a skewer to make the start of a hole.*

ABOVE: **1** *Collect together all the pieces to make the posy and spread them out. Cut off any leaves and lower branches to leave the stems clear.*

ABOVE: **2** *Begin to make the posy in one hand, adding one flower at a time, with the other free hand mixing the colours and varieties equally.*

RIGHT: *A posy like this one makes a lovely gift and needs no extra arranging once received. It will stand in a vase or glass in water just as it is.*

ABOVE: **3** *Continue adding more flowers, keeping the posy in a neat shape. Do not worry about the stems at this stage.*

ABOVE: **4** *Once the posy is complete tie it tightly around the stems with fine wire a little way down from the flower heads.*

ABOVE: **5** *Now trim off the base of the stems using secateurs or shape scissors to give a neat even finish. Tie a ribbon bow to cover the wire.*

Phlox

*P*hlox are lovely summer cut flowers which look good in arrangements mixed with all the other seasonal material available. They are commonly perennial plants, although there are annual species, and often grown in gardens, where they make excellent herbaceous border flowers with their mass of flowers above strong straight stems. Original versions were pink but there are many colours now available.

Early glasshouse crops are available in spring and then phlox are around for the whole summer, though some are coming from growers in Israel now through the autumn and winter. Generally the flower heads are a single colour but there are also types with a ring of contrasting colour in the centre. There are mauves and all shades of pink, scarlet and claret-red, white, purple, violet-blue and even bright salmon-orange.

Phlox are useful cut flowers for large-scale arrangements as they have very straight stiff stems up to a metre in length. When purchased the first few flowers of the cluster should be open, then later the rest will do so. A few flowers may drop or can be pinched off while new ones develop. In this way, the blooms should last for up to ten days.

ABOVE: **1** *This strong blue pot makes a good colour contrast to the mixed flowers used in it. Cut damp floral foam and wedge it inside the pot.*

RIGHT: **2** *Trim the stems off a mixture of white gypsophila and blue annual delphinium. These are used as a frothy filler to the arrangement.*

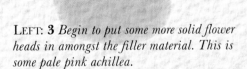

LEFT: *This is a simple and traditional full arrangement using summer garden flowers, but the pot gives it an unexpected edge and an up-to-date look.*

LEFT: **3** *Begin to put some more solid flower heads in amongst the filler material. This is some pale pink achillea.*

LEFT: **4** *Now put some stems of a bright pink phlox into the arrangement. Spread these out equally and put some shorter stems at the edges.*

ABOVE: **5** *Finally, use some paler coloured phlox as well as the shocking pink ones to finish off the arrangement. Use mauve and soft pink.*

Phlox

BELOW: **1** *Stand a round glass goldfish bowl or vase on three square sheets of bright tissue paper. The layers should not correspond particularly.*

BELOW: **2** *Gather the paper up and around the neck of the vase. Be bold and quick to minimize unwanted creases. Tie paper with wire or string.*

ABOVE: *Scrunch the paper into any shape you like to make a pretty frame to the flowers. This idea would work a variety of different arrangements.*

BELOW: **4** *Now add several stems of pale mauve scabious, spacing them out amongst the antirrhinums. Use about fifteen blooms.*

LEFT: **3** *Fill vase with water first and then begin to add flowers. First put some spikes of red antirrhinums spaced around the edge.*

ABOVE: **5** *Now to complete the arrangement add sprays of bright pink and pal mauve phlox throughout the other flowers. Cut them at slightly different heights.*

ABOVE: **1** *Using two containers of slightly different sizes makes an unusual arrangement. Fill both with a block of damp foam.*

ABOVE: **2** *Work on both baskets together and fill the foam with sprays of eucalyptus to make a foliage background for the flowers.*

ABOVE: **3** *When both baskets have their foliage, start to add flowers. Here a deep red sweet pea is added to the eucalyptus.*

LEFT: **4** *Add more sweet peas in burgundy and white and then start to put some phlox in amongst them. Cut their stems quite short.*

RIGHT: **5** *Put in enough phlox to make the baskets look full but not crowded, with a good balance of flowers to foliage.*

BELOW: *Stand the two baskets side by side or one slightly in front of the other. They would look pretty on a polished wood surface.*

Waxflowers

A fairly recent arrival in the world of cut flowers is the pretty and versatile Waxflower or, to give it its botanical name, Chamelaucium uncinatum. Confusingly it is sometimes known as Waxplant too. Originally an Australian plant, most supplies are now grown in Israel and it is available more or less all the year round with the peak of its production during the winter months.

It is sold in bunches of one colour and the foliage has a faintly aromatic and citrus fragrance when crushed or cut. The small star-shaped flowers are clustered near the ends of the branches and come in a soft pink, greenish white or deeper mauvish pink versions. The leather leaves are narrow and pointed like small needles.

Waxflower is extremely long lasting in water, keeping up to two weeks or more. A bunch goes a long way split up into many smaller pieces so it is a good filler to put with other materials, especially when flowers are expensive during the winter months. A large bowl filled with waxflower alone could look very pretty but it is more likely to be combined with other flowers.

ABOVE: **1** *You need a medium sized floral foam ball well soaked. Push a stick right through the axis and leave it in place to hold on to while arranging.*

RIGHT: *Wind a little small-leaved ivy around the hanging string, then attach this to whatever you wish to hang the ball from. Trim off excess string.*

ABOVE: **2** *Start to push flower heads all over the ball, turning it as you go. The flower stems should be very short.*

ABOVE: **3** *Continue adding large flower heads across the whole ball and then fill any gaps in the foam with small bunches of waxflower.*

ABOVE: **4** *When the ball is completely and densely covered with flowers attach a piece of string to the stick.*

ABOVE: **5** *Pull the stick clear of the ball and the string will follow. Leave extra string at the bottom of the ball and remove the stick.*

ABOVE: **6** *Tie a small piece of twig to string at bottom of the ball, then pull string back up. The stick will sit across the hole.*

Waxflowers

ABOVE: **1** *Take a black plastic flowerpot and glue cinnamon sticks level with base and 3 cm (1¼ in) or so above top edge.*

ABOVE: **2** *When there are cinnamon sticks right the way round the pot, twine a length of ivy round the middle and wire it together at the back.*

ABOVE: **3** *Put a block of damp floral foam into the pot and then begin to put small sprigs of waxflower all over the foam.*

ABOVE: **4** *Snip away any stray or straggling leaves that are above the general level of the waxflowers in the pot using secateurs or scissors.*

LEFT: *This makes a very unusual and pretty autumn or winter arrangement making the most of a few roses. Re-use the cinnamon decorated pot over and over again.*

ABOVE: **5** *Finally, add some deep cerise pink roses all round the pot in amongst the waxflowers. Five blooms should be enough.*

RIGHT: *Stand the completed posies together in a simple glass container filled with water. The leaves will support the posies on the vase edge.*

BELOW: **1** *Cut a branch of waxflower into several smaller pieces. Do the same with some Michaelmas daisies. Collect some vine leaves.*

BELOW: **3** *Add another sprig of waxflower to the posy and then a piece of Michaelmas daisy. This should be enough to make one posy.*

ABOVE: **2** *Using a vine leaf as a collar, hold it in one hand and begin to make a little posy. Start with a sprig of waxflower.*

RIGHT: **4** *Tie the posy with fine wire to hold it together. Make another three or more posies in the same way.*

Daffodils

Daffodils are the great spring flower, bringing sunshine and colour to any arrangement, simple or grand. As they are so commonly grown in gardens they are often underrated as cut flowers, but they last well in water and are normally inexpensive to buy and always plentiful from winter right through the spring season. There is a vast range of varieties available, offering different colours, sizes and shapes of bloom.

Most varieties are bright golden yellow but there are some types with clusters of smaller scented flowers such as 'Paperwhite' and 'Cheerfulness' narcissi with cream or white blooms.

Normally sold in tight bud, daffodils quickly open out in warm and light conditions and last for up to twelve days. The cut stems give off a slime which can taint the water that they are in, so change the water every day or so if possible. Generous bunches of daffodils displayed on their own in a plain vase or a basket are simple and always pretty but the flowers can be mixed with other materials, though only in medium to small-scale arrangements as the stems are never very long.

ABOVE: **1** *For this idea you will need two different sized baskets lined at their bases and filled with damp floral foam*

ABOVE: 2 *The foam must fit neatly and tightly into the baskets as the flower stems will go right to the edges. Make the foam level with the top of the basket.*

ABOVE: 3 *Put the small basket in front of the larger one. Now start to put daffodils into the large basket, working across from one side to the other.*

ABOVE: *This is a simple but very stylish way of displaying daffodils without using many pieces. Stand the baskets on a mantelpiece, narrow table or shelf.*

LEFT: 4 *Continue until the basket is filled. Now put smaller daffodils into the front basket. These are cut quite short.*

RIGHT: 5 *Finish off the arrangement by putting a layer of moss around the stems in the larger basket to hide the exposed foam.*

ABOVE: **1** *Another idea needing two colour-related containers of different sizes. First put a bunch of solidago in the large jug.*

ABOVE: **2** *Next add a bunch of yellow ranunculus. Work using small bunches rather than single blooms for the right effect.*

LEFT: The combination of yellow with blue always looks very fresh and appealing, especially with a little contrasting white, but you could use green jugs if preferred.

LEFT: **3** *Finally, add a small bunch of white tulips to give a colour contrast. Loosen out the bunches of flowers slightly.*

RIGHT: **4** *Now work on the smaller jug which will stand in front of the group. Begin with a bunch of scented cream narcissi.*

ABOVE: **5** *Add a bunch of yellow ranunculus in front and to one side of the narcissi. Then add a final bunch of daffodils.*

RIGHT: **2** *Continue adding flowers, mixing the colours and varieties of types throughout the wreath and working round in one direction.*

ABOVE: **1** *Using a foam base makes wreath construction very quick and easy. Soak the ring thoroughly before starting to put small flowers and leaves in place.*

ABOVE: **3** *When you have covered right round to the start check that the inner edge is well covered. Fix a wire loop to the back for hanging the wreath.*

RIGHT: *This wreath is designed primarily for hanging from a door or wall but it can be laid flat and used as a table centrepiece.*

Chrysanthemums

*T*hese must be the most widely sold and used cut flowers in the world. Because they are so long lived they have always been popular with florists and therefore have become rather a cliché. They need not be if they are used in imaginative ways. The types most commonly seen are those varieties which can be grown all the year round. Chrysanthemums can last for up to three weeks in fresh water.

Garden chrysanthemums are slightly more interesting and less uniform but they are only available for picking in late autumn. They tend to have large mop-head flowers or clusters of many small double flowers. The florist varieties vary too, with some having single blooms on long stems and the highly popular single-flowered types with several flowers on branching stems looking like daisies. The colour range is vast with all the typical oranges, bronzes and yellows as well as mauves, pinks, peaches and whites. New versions with decorative quilled or ragged petals are sometimes seen as well as spider types which have very narrow long petals.

Clean leaves off lower stems before arranging chrysanthemums.

ABOVE: **1** *The vase you use for this should be quite tall and it must have a neck. Stand it on a square of silk or stiff cotton.*

ABOVE: **2** *Bring fabric up and and around the sides of the vase. Tie tightly round the neck of the vase with string or ribbon.*

ABOVE: **3** *Roll back the excess fabric at the top of the vase to make a kind of ring or collar, tucking the raw edges under.*

BELOW: **5** *Now add lilies and some terracotta-coloured freesias, spreading them out evenly amongst the other flowers.*

ABOVE: *This idea makes a very elegant and unusual arrangement and, of course, can be varied, depending on the types and colours of flowers and fabric used.*

LEFT: **4** *Clean off any foliage and small branches from the stems of the spray chrysanthemums. Re-cut stems and place in vase.*

Chrysanthemums

ABOVE: **1** *For this arrangement you will need a foam ball of medium size. Soak it very well in a bowl of water until damp right through.*

ABOVE: **2** *Wrap a piece of gold cord right round the circumference of the ball. Twist a piece of wire round the cord to hold it in place.*

ABOVE: **3** *Cut several chrysanthemums into separate heads with very short stems. Push them into the foam ball in a row alternating the different colours.*

RIGHT: *Chrysanthemums make the ideal flowers for this kind of arrangement. Tough and easy to use, they make very long-lasting decorations like this one.*

ABOVE: **4** *Towards the end of adding flower heads it is easier to hang the ball from the cord and to continue working this way.*

ABOVE: **5** *Finally, make a bow from gold wire-edged ribbon and attach a short piece of stub wire to its centre. Push the wire into the ball where the cord starts.*

ABOVE: **1** *Twist a few stems of small-leaved ivy around a ready-made vine twig wreath. Tuck in the ends of the ivy stems to hide them.*

ABOVE: **2** *Lay the wreath on a flat surface, then half-fill a glass vase with water and stand it in the centre of the ivy-decorated vine wreath.*

LEFT: **3** *Clean the stems of dahlias and chrysanthemum so that there is no foliage left on them. Mix the two types of flowers equally in the vase.*

ABOVE: *This quick and easy idea transforms a plain glass vase into a spectacular arrangement. You could use an opaque vase instead of glass.*

Chrysanthemums

BELOW: **1** *You will need three small flattish pumpkins or squashes. Twist lengths of small-leaved ivy to make little garlands.*

LEFT: **2** *Put an ivy garland around the tops of each squash. The garlands should be small enough not to slip down over the fattest part.*

ABOVE: **3** *Prepare some chrysanthemums to add to the ivy. Snip the flower heads off the stems leaving just a tiny part of the stalk.*

ABOVE: **4** *Tuck the flowers into the ivy garlands, putting one flower on one squash, two on the next and three on the third. Add a dill or fennel flower.*

ABOVE: *This little group would make a lovely autumn table decoration for a dinner party or special meal. Stand them on a tray, a pretty plate or mat.*

ABOVE: 1 *You will need a length of strong but soft wire to thread pieces on to. Cut chrysanthemum flower heads completely off stems.*

You can twist the threaded wire and make a small circular wreath like this one or thread more pieces onto the wire and make a long garland.

ABOVE: 2 *Push a length of wire through the centre of a flower head. You should put each subsequent flower on the wire facing in the same direction.*

RIGHT: 3 *Now thread a dried eucalyptus leaf onto the wire and then three or four more. Hang fresh eucalyptus in a warm place for a few days, then strip off leaves.*

RIGHT: 4 *Next add dried apple rings or a similar dried fruit and then continue threading pieces until you have a long garland.*

Celosia

Celosia is a strange and exotic addition to the choice of cut flowers. Its curled velvet cockscomb heads are unlike any other flower and look as if they are a manmade material though they are in fact a plant originally found growing wild in Tropical Africa. The scarlet version is seen most commonly but they come in yellow, red and purple too. Celosia's vivid colour and solid shape will always add drama and excitement to an arrangement, however simple it may be in design.

The strange flower sits at the top of a strong tall stem with a few soft leaves below it. These are normally taken off before using the bloom. Celosia cristata is generally available from late spring through to the autumn and generally grown under glass, though some from Kenya is grown outdoors. Celosia plumosa is a similar plant but the silky flowers grow in a tall plume shape.

Take care not to drop water on the velvety flowers of celosia as they spot and stain very easily. Cut the stems and split them a little way before arranging them in water with cut flower food added. They should last up to ten days. Celosia dries very well, keeping its colour better than many flowers.

ABOVE: **1** *Line a shallow oblong basket with foil or plastic to make it waterproof. Fill the basket with damp floral foam half-way up the sides.*

ABOVE: **2** *Cut stems of fresh celosia and green sedum with short stems. Push them into the foam, mixing them equally.*

ABOVE: **3** *Make triple loops with short lengths of ribbon. This red gingham shows up well with the red and green of the flowers.*

RIGHT: **4** *Twist a short piece of stub wire round the base of the ribbon, gathering the loops and holding them in place to make little rosettes.*

ABOVE: **5** *Push the finished ribbon rosettes in amongst the sedum and celosia, spreading them out evenly throughout the arrangement.*

LEFT: *This makes a very effective yet simple arrangement. The brilliant red of the celosia needs the cool contrast of the green to offset it.*

89

Celosia

ABOVE: **1** *For this bouquet the green contrast to the red is provided by leaving some of the upper leaves in place of the stem. Remove the lower ones.*

ABOVE: *A magnificent and vibrant bouquet to present to someone or to attach to a door.*

RIGHT: **5** *Make a small bow with wire-edged ribbon and attach it to a wire. Tuck this into the tartan bow and push the wire out of sight.*

ABOVE: **2** *Make a bouquet by starting with one stem in one hand and adding subsequent stems with the other, fanning them out slightly.*

ABOVE: **3** *The bunch will get quite heavy so lay it down and tie the stems with wire to hold them together.*

ABOVE: **4** *Wrap a long length of narrow tartan ribbon round the stems to hide the wire. Tie this into a bow.*

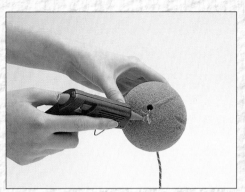

ABOVE: **1** *For this idea you will need an electric glue gun or suitable adhesive. Push a stick through a dried foam ball.*

ABOVE: **2** *Thread a decorative cord through the hole in the ball and keep it from slipping through with a blob of glue.*

ABOVE: **3** *Now, using plenty of hot glue, start to attach pieces of dried celosia over the ball. Hold them until the glue has set.*

ABOVE: **4** *Continue adding more pieces all over the ball, leaving equal spaces between them to attach other pieces later.*

ABOVE: **5** *Now push small sprigs of dried and dyed eucalyptus in amongst the celosia. They probably will not need to be glued.*

ABOVE: *Finish off by putting some deep red dried roses in amongst the other pieces to make a long-lasting and attractive dried decoration.*

Asters

Asters are an old fashioned flower, often forgotten about these days with so much exotic material around but they are excellent cut flowers, plentiful and inexpensive. Their shaggy heads are like large daisies or chrysanthemums. The aster family of flowers is huge and includes Michaelmas daisies but what we call Asters are just one type from this big group. Asters are an annual flower and are available from mid summer onwards with a peak of supplies at the end of summer and early autumn.

There are many types of Aster available, including some singles and others with very curly petals and some with more globular-shaped blooms. They are always sold as mixtures in bunches of carmine red, violet, pink and white.

Aster stems are quite short with a few little leaves along them. Remove these and always keep a check on the water that the flowers are in. It quickly gets polluted by the stems so should be changed often. Asters mix well with many other summer flowers but, as the stems are short, asters do have limited use and are confined to small and medium arrangements. They can last up to two weeks

ABOVE: **1** *An antique basket becomes the container for this lovely summer mixture. Line the base and fill the basket with damp floral foam.*

BELOW: *This basket manages to look sumptuous and elaborate though it is made from very ordinary and simple flowers. The brown basket looks lovely with the pinks and reds.*

ABOVE: **2** *Put some tall spikes of Michaelmas daisy into the foam to set an outline. Next add some sedum heads.*

RIGHT: **3** *Now put some small stems of spray chrysanthemums in amongst the sedum. Keep the level of the solid flowers just below the handle height.*

FAR RIGHT: **4** *Finish the arrangement with several double asters, using shades of pink only. Mix the different sizes and colours throughout.*

ABOVE: **5** *To complete the old-fashioned look, tie a soft ribbon to trail from the point where the basket handle joins the front edge.*

Asters

BELOW: **1** *This really could not be simpler to put together. The trick is in choosing a flower combination. Put water and clear glass marbles in a square tank.*

ABOVE: **2** *The glass marbles help hold stems in place where there is no foam or wire. Add some raspberry pink Michaelmas daisies.*

ABOVE: **3** *A pale dusky mauve late-summer allium is cut to length and added throughout the Michaelmas daisies.*

ABOVE: **4** *The marbles mean that you can place each flower quite precisely. Make the blooms at the front of the vase slightly shorter than the back ones.*

RIGHT: *A simple, but classic, arrangement which is the kind of useful vase of flowers that would look good anywhere in the house during the late summer.*

LEFT: **5** *Now finish off with some rich purple asters taken from a mixed bunch or from the garden. They should be roughly equal in quantity to the pink daisies.*

RIGHT: **1** *Use a dahlia or similar flower as the central flower to the posy. Surround it with some pieces of pale green and white euphorbia marginata.*

BELOW: **2** *Now continue building up the posy by adding several short stems of deep blue delphinium around the euphorbia.*

ABOVE: **3** *Build up the posy by adding asters in shades of pink, dark and light. Work round the posy until you reach the start.*

LEFT: **4** *A few smaller flowers can be added. These are small-flowered spray chrysanthemums with a pretty darker eye.*

BELOW: *The finished posy is simple but very attractive. Although the flowers are not exotic it would make a lovely bouquet for a bridesmaid.*

BELOW: **6** *Finally, a special bow is added. This two-tone wire-edged ribbon in blue makes the perfect choice, contrasting with the pink flowers.*

LEFT: **5** *Tie the stems tightly together to make a handle for the posy, then trim each stem neatly. They do have to be even in length.*

Scabious

Scabious are summer flowering in the garden, but are grown commercially to spread their season from late spring into the autumn these days. They are a pretty pale mauve-blue which mixes very well with many other flowers. Scabious are usually sold in bunches, not singly, and to be fresh should be only half-open. Scabious should last in water for up to twelve days if kept fresh and water replenished and topped up.

Cut stems and remove any little leaves and extra buds on the lower stems. Alongside the main flowers in each bunch there are usually plenty of unopened buds too. Keep these or not, depending on the style of arrangement that you intend to make but do not expect many of these buds to open out because they have been cut too young.

The stems of scabious are straight but not particularly strong or long, so they are not suitable for really large-scale arrangements. The simple flower shape and attractive colour makes scabious a deservedly popular cut flower but it is generally used with other pieces rather than as a specimen flower on its own.

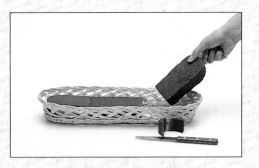

ABOVE: **1** *Use a very narrow long and shallow basket such as one for French bread. Fill it with damp floral foam right up to the edges.*

ABOVE: **2** *Now begin to add sprigs of a spike-shaped flower such as this apple mint along the middle of the basket. These set the size and outline.*

ABOVE: **3** *Next put some softer filler material such as this white lace flower cut with short stems in a row across the basket.*

RIGHT: **4** *Pale pink lavatera and purplish pink stokesia are placed next at random through the other flowers, facing them forward where possible.*

ABOVE: **5** *Finally, finish off by adding the scabious flowers throughout the arrangement. About twelve were used here.*

LEFT: *The narrowness from front to back of this arrangement makes it ideal for a shelf or ledge with little depth or to fit into a window sill.*

Scabious

LEFT: **3** *When the lavender edging is complete trim the top of it with scissors so that it is in a perfect straight line.*

ABOVE: **4** *Now make a row of three carnations from front to back at the left side of the basket, pushing the heads down close to the foam and level with the lavender.*

RIGHT: *The pretty paper collar makes a very simple arrangement look more exciting. You could use paper doilies in different colours or a gold foil version.*

BELOW: **1** *You will need to use a narrow-necked jar to take the posy and a silver paper doily. Cut a piece of double-sided tape ready for next stage.*

ABOVE: **4** *Then begin to put flowers in place one at a time. Here scabious are mixed with nerines.*

ABOVE: **3** *The doily should stay in place, especially once flowers are in the vase. Pinch the paper into a few folds. Add some water.*

ABOVE: **5** *Put the second row of carnations in place on the other side of the basket and then in-fill with the scabious heads.*

ABOVE: **2** *Cut doily to middle and cut out centre to the size of the vase. Overlap doily into a slight cone shape and tape edges together.*

Lilies

A vailable all the year round nowadays, lilies are justifiably popular as exotic and luxurious cut flowers. Many hybrids have been developed providing a vast range of colours and there are several flower shapes to choose from. Renowned for their wonderful fragrance, a few stems of certain varieties can scent a whole room. All lilies are long stemmed and last for up to ten days as cut flowers.

Three main types of lily are available. Easter lilies with very long white trumpets and a rich perfume are one kind. The second group are also scented and are the Oriental hybrids such as 'Stargazer' and 'Casablanca'. Third, there are the 'Mid-Century' hybrids with flatter, more open flowers, no scent, and a wide colour range from deep plum red to brilliant golden yellow.

Once open the flowers have large pollen-laden stamens. These can be removed if there is a risk of pollen staining fabrics or furniture. Lilies are often sold in quite tight bud but each flower will open in sequence and dead blooms can be removed as required.

ABOVE: **1** *Prepare some long-stemmed red roses and some 'Stargazer' lilies. Trim off any lower leaves from the roses and lilies.*

ABOVE: 2 *Cut off the lower leaves of some euphoria marginata and gather together red roses, 'Stargazer' lilies and white amaryllis.*

ABOVE: 3 *Start to make the bouquet in your hand. An amaryllis should be the basis with some euphorbia added to it. Next include a rose, then lily and so on.*

LEFT: *The combination of pink and white lilies and white amaryllis with deep red roses and variegated foliage is dramatic and bold. The dark green ribbon makes a good foil.*

LEFT: 4 *When the bouquet is full and complete tie wire around the stems just under the flowers and then trim off the stems to a comfortable length.*

RIGHT: 5 *Now wrap an openweave ribbon to cover the wire and make a large loose bow with short ends. Pull the loops out to look as full as possible.*

Lilies

LEFT: **1** *This makes use of orange lilies and autumn berries such as these whitebeam berries. Trim off leaves, leaving just berries on bare branches.*

RIGHT: **2** *Clean off the lower leaves which cluster at the base of lily stems. No foliage is required for this particular arrangement.*

ABOVE: **3** *Use a suitable narrow-necked vase filled with water and begin to put the berried branches in place to make a basic framework.*

RIGHT: *The colours in this arrangement are vibrant and bold and typical of the autumn season. Combining flowers with berries shows how adaptable lilies are.*

RIGHT: **4** *Now add the lilies, using the branches of whitebeam as a support. Try to face most of the lily blooms towards the front in this arrangement.*

RIGHT: **1** *Just one or two lily heads are exotic enough to make a great display. Pile some different fruits onto a stemmed dish.*

FAR RIGHT: **2** *Complete the fruit pyramid, then tuck some small clusters of rose hips or berries in amongst the polished fruits.*

BELOW: **3** *Now take four lily flower heads cut from a single stem and push them in amongst the fruit, facing them in different directions.*

BELOW: *The finished fruit bowl will look wonderful standing in pride of place on a sideboard or dining table.*

RIGHT: **4** *Finally, for a colour contrast, add a spray or two of foliage to set off the fruits and flowers.*

Carnations

*C*arnations are so well known that they hardly need any description. Two main types are sold as cut flowers, the large-headed flowers known just as carnations, and the branched spray carnations with many small flowers and buds on a single stem. There are also summer varieties available from florists, such as 'Doris' pinks, which are more like outdoor garden-grown pinks or dianthus.

They have become ubiquitous in bouquets and arrangements because they are such a long-lived flower. Spray carnations are usually split up into single flowers and used for wedding decorations, posies and similar arrangements. Large carnations can be a little difficult to use and are not very interesting on their own. They tend to look better with a good mixture of other seasonal material, which makes one forget that they are available all year.

Colours are not especially subtle but there is a huge range from white, cream, pink and peach, lemon yellow, deep red, scarlet and burgundy. There are some varieties with different coloured edges or stripes. They can last for up to sixteen days.

ABOVE: **1** *This classic vase makes arranging a formal design easy. Wedge in a piece of damp floral foam, leaving plenty above the top of the vase.*

LEFT: *The large pink carnations fill out the final design and give it solidity and substance. It would look good in any room.*

ABOVE LEFT: **2** *Begin to put some large decorative foliage at the back and sides of the foam. They will set the scale and shape.*

LEFT: **3** *Add some smaller branches of foliage such as viburnum, putting a few shorter pieces at the front of the arrangement.*

ABOVE: **4** *Michaelmas daisies and mauve statice add areas of colour throughout the arrangement and hellebores provide a different texture. Put the first carnations in place.*

105

Carnations

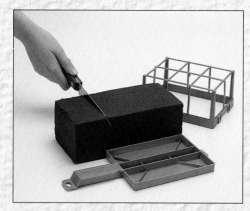

RIGHT: *Finish off the pew end arrangement with a ribbon and bow, if you like, and attach with a strong wire loop to the pew or wall. The whole block is very heavy.*

ABOVE: **1** *For this pew end or hanging arrangement you will need a special plastic container. Cut damp floral foam to fit the base.*

RIGHT: **2** *Push the foam into the base, then snap the lid over it. It should lock itself tightly shut. A standard foam block will have the right proportions.*

BELOW: **3** *Hang the frame in a vertical position so that it is possible to see it as it will eventually be. Start to add some long stems of ivy.*

BELOW: **4** *Add smaller pieces of variegated euonymus and green hellebore flowers in the centre of the foam block so that the whole shape is covered with foliage.*

BELOW: **5** *Now put small sprigs of mauve statice and Michaelmas daisies in amongst the foliage background. Make sure the sides are covered too.*

BELOW: **6** *Take a bunch of apricot spray carnations and split up into lots of single flower heads. Put these into the arrangement, spreading them out evenly.*

RIGHT: *This kind of arrangement is most effective seen from above so that the pattern and rings of colour are most obvious.*

ABOVE: **1** *This ready-made foam block sits in its own saucer. Put one carnation in the centre, then a ring of daisies round it.*

ABOVE: **2** *Now make the next ring of flowers using spray carnations in a pale orange colour. Put them very close together.*

ABOVE: **3** *Make the next ring in spray carnations of a slightly different colour. Finish off with small sprigs of variegated foliage.*

Carnations

BELOW: **1** *Cut a piece of damp floral foam to fit a small heart-shaped basket. Line the basket first with a piece of plastic. Put one red rose in the centre.*

LEFT: **2** *Next make a ring of pink carnations round the red rose. Put the flowers as close together as possible. Now add a row of paler pink tulips.*

ABOVE: **3** *Finish the edge with pink genista and make curls of shiny pink ribbon. Add wires to ribbons and push into arrangement.*

LEFT: *This would make a lovely Valentine gift. Carnations are ideal for this kind of design as they are so uniform in colour, shape and size.*

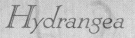Hydrangea

Roses

Carnations

Mimosa

lies

Euphorbia

esias

Orchids

Tiger Lilies

Delphiniums

Violets

Ivy

Irises

Daffodils

Tulips

onies

Anemones